THE NEW ALPHABET
OF ANIMALS

A

B

C

D

E

F

G

H

I

J

K

L

M

N

O

P

Q

R

S

T
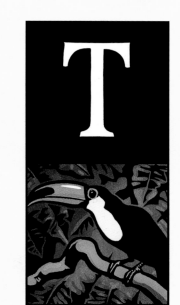

U

V

W

X

Y

Z

THE NEW ALPHABET OF ANIMALS

BY CHRISTOPHER WORMELL

RUNNING PRESS

PHILADELPHIA · LONDON

Printed in China

9   8   7   6   5   4   3   2   1
Digit on the right indicates the number of this printing

Library of Congress Cataloging-in-Publication Number 2002100475

ISBN 0-7624-1347-6

Cover and interior design by Dustin Summers
Edited by Melissa Wagner
Typography: Caslon

This book may be ordered by mail from the publisher. Please include $2.50 for postage and handling.
But try your bookstore first!

Running Press Book Publishers
125 South Twenty-second Street
Philadelphia, Pennsylvania 19103-4399

Visit us on the web!
www.runningpress.com

For Mary

Armadillo

Bb

Buffalo

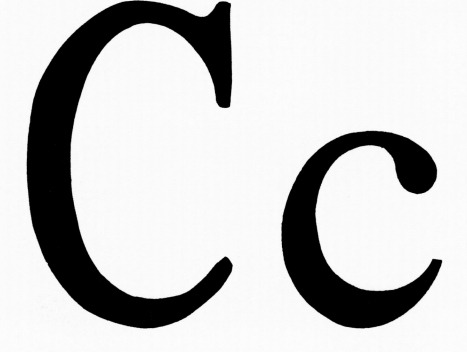

Camel

Dolphin

Eagle

Ff

Fox

Gorilla

Horse

Ii

Ibex

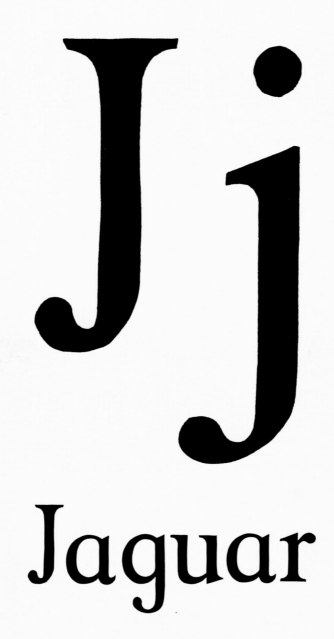

Jaguar

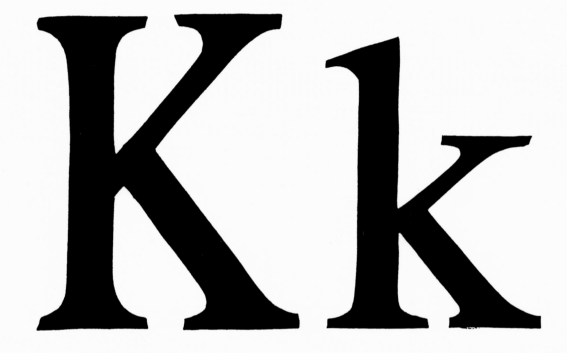

Kk

Kingfisher

L l

Lion

Mouse

Newt

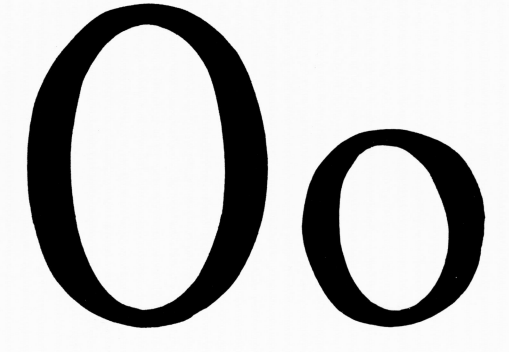

Owl

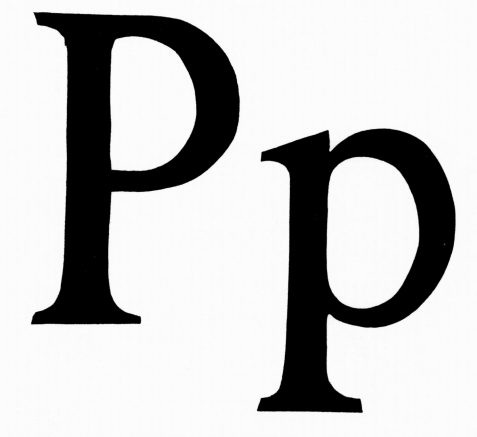

Penguin

Quail

Rr

Raccoon

Ss

Sheep

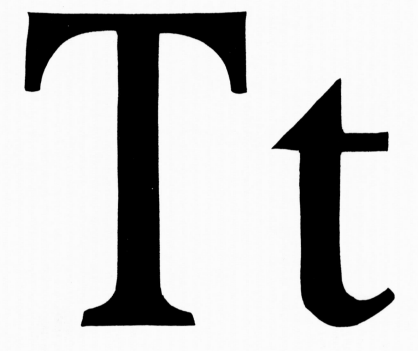

Toucan

Uakari

Viper

Ww

Woodpecker

Xx

Xenops

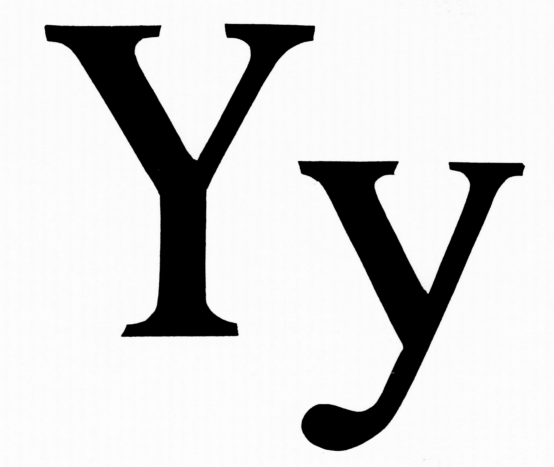

Yellowhammer

Zz

Zorilla

SOME OF THE LESS FAMILIAR ANIMALS FEATURED IN THIS BOOK INCLUDE:

IBEX: A wild goat that lives high among the snowy peaks of the Alps in Switzerland, Italy, and North Africa.

KINGFISHER: A small, brilliantly colored bird with a large beak that lives by streams and rivers catching small fish and other aquatic creatures.

UAKARI: A bald-faced monkey found in Brazil that lives in the tree-tops of the rain forest and feeds mainly on fruit.

XENOPS: A small insect-eating bird that nests in holes in dead trees in Central and South America.

YELLOWHAMMER: A small European bird found in open grass-land and farmland where it feeds on seeds, grains, berries, and leaves.

ZORILLA: A nocturnal animal of the African savanna that, like the skunk, releases a foul odor when alarmed.

Christopher Wormell is a leading English wood engraver. Inspired by the works of Thomas Bewick, he took up wood engraving in 1982, and has since illustrated several books in addition to his work in the fields of advertising, design, and editorial illustration.

Long before Christopher became a wood engraver he was taught lino-cutting by his father, mainly for the mass production of Christmas cards. Around Christmastime the Wormell household became something of a cottage industry with Christopher and his brothers and sisters producing handmade cards by the hundred.

His first book for children, *An Alphabet of Animals*, started as a series of simple, colorful lino-cut illustrations for his son Jack, and eventually grew into a book that took the Graphics Prize at the Bologna International Children's Book Fair in 1991. Some of Christopher's other children's book credits include *Mowgli's Brothers*, *Blue Rabbit and Friends*, *Blue Rabbit and the Runaway Wheel*, *Animal Train*, *Off to the Fair*, and *George and the Dragon*.

He lives in London with his wife and three children.

a
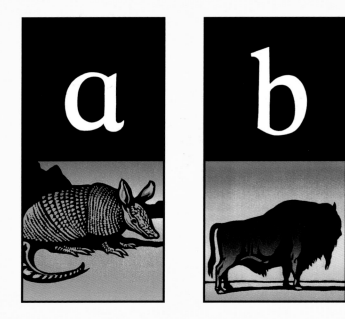

b

c

d

e

f

g

h
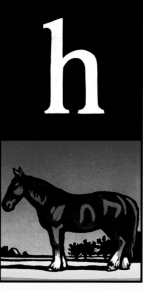

i

j
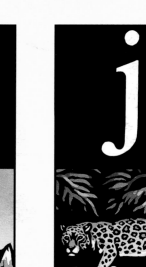

k

l

m

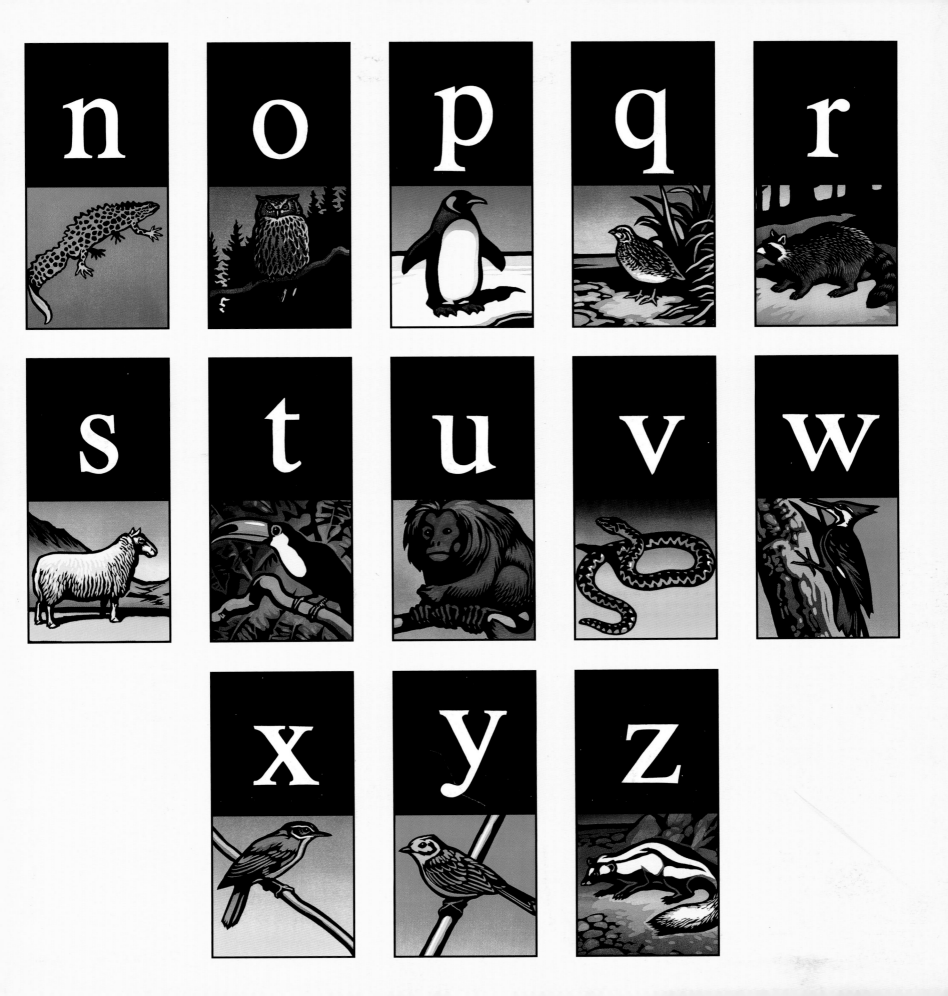